MW01001053

This book belongs to:

- -

- -

Unwind Every Day

a journal

CHRONICLE BOOKS

SAN FRANCISCO

ISBN 978-1-4521-6781-7

Manufactured in China

MIX
Paper from
responsible sources
FSC™ C008047

Designed and illustrated by Allison Weiner

Chronicle Books publishes distinctive books and gifts. From
award-winning children's titles, bestselling cookbooks, and
eclectic pop culture to acclaimed works of art and design,
stationery, and journals, we craft publishing that's instantly
recognizable for its spirit and creativity. Enjoy our publishing and
become part of our community at www.chroniclebooks.com.

10 9 8 7 6 5 4 3 2

Chronicle Books LLC
680 Second Street
San Francisco, CA 94107
www.chroniclebooks.com

Special quantity discounts are available to corporations and
other organizations. Contact our premiums department at
corporatesales@chroniclebooks.com or at 1-800-759-0190.

This book could not have been created without the
thoughtful contributions of:

Alexandra Brown, Alice Chau, Allison Weiner, Amy Cleary,
Amy Treadwell, Deanne Katz, Freesia Blizard, Jennifer
Tolo Pierce, Madeline Moe, Natalie Beaulieu, Pippa White,
Rachel Hiles, Sara Waitt, Sarah Billingsley, Tera Killip,
Vanessa Dina, and Zaneta Jung

Introduction

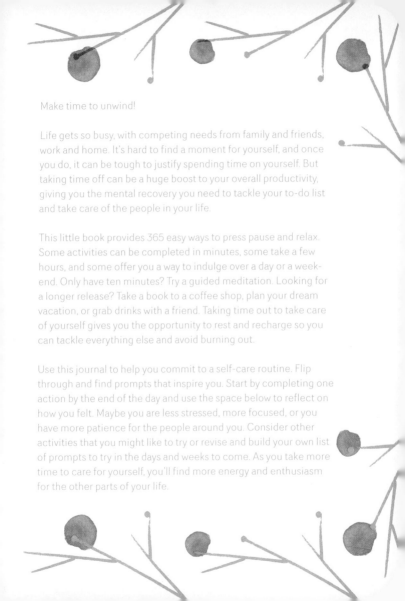

Make time to unwind!

Life gets so busy, with competing needs from family and friends, work and home. It's hard to find a moment for yourself, and once you do, it can be tough to justify spending time on yourself. But taking time off can be a huge boost to your overall productivity, giving you the mental recovery you need to tackle your to-do list and take care of the people in your life.

This little book provides 365 easy ways to press pause and relax. Some activities can be completed in minutes, some take a few hours, and some offer you a way to indulge over a day or a weekend. Only have ten minutes? Try a guided meditation. Looking for a longer release? Take a book to a coffee shop, plan your dream vacation, or grab drinks with a friend. Taking time out to take care of yourself gives you the opportunity to rest and recharge so you can tackle everything else and avoid burning out.

Use this journal to help you commit to a self-care routine. Flip through and find prompts that inspire you. Start by completing one action by the end of the day and use the space below to reflect on how you felt. Maybe you are less stressed, more focused, or you have more patience for the people around you. Consider other activities that you might like to try or revise and build your own list of prompts to try in the days and weeks to come. As you take more time to care for yourself, you'll find more energy and enthusiasm for the other parts of your life.

Call a friend

COMPLETED ON ....

REFLECT ....

....

....

Plan something fun for the weekend

COMPLETED ON ....

REFLECT ....

....

....

Wander
around

your neighborhood

COMPLETED ON ....

REFLECT ....

....

....

Look at photos or videos

of cute animals

COMPLETED ON ....

REFLECT ....

....

....

Write down whatever comes into your mind

for the next five minutes

COMPLETED ON ....

REFLECT ....

....

....

Ask a friend for a TV for a TV show or movie

recommendation and then watch it

COMPLETED ON ....

REFLECT ....

....

....

Treat yourself to your

favorite coffee shop drink or snack

COMPLETED ON Nov 3 ❤

REFLECT Salir de la cama y venir a estudiar para PHR.

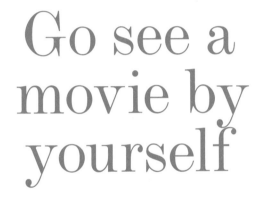

Go see a movie by yourself

COMPLETED ON ....

REFLECT ....

....

....

Get in bed early and read

COMPLETED ON ....

REFLECT ....

....

....

Make yourself a playlist

COMPLETED ON ....

REFLECT ....

....

....

Say "no" to something

COMPLETED ON ....

REFLECT ....

....

....

Write down ten compliments for yourself.

Talk to yourself like you would to a friend

COMPLETED ON ....

REFLECT ....

....

....

Lounge around the house

in fuzzy slippers

COMPLETED ON ....

REFLECT ....

....

....

Buy yourself a new book

COMPLETED ON ....

REFLECT ....

....

....

Pour yourself a glass of wine

COMPLETED ON ....

REFLECT ....

....

....

Doodle for ten minutes

COMPLETED ON ....

REFLECT ....

....

....

Play your favorite song.

Hit repeat

COMPLETED ON ....

REFLECT ....

....

....

Find a sunny spot

COMPLETED ON ....

REFLECT ....

....

....

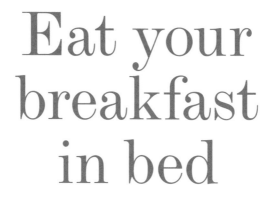

Eat your breakfast in bed

COMPLETED ON ....

REFLECT ....

....

....

Put on a cute temporary tattoo

COMPLETED ON ....

REFLECT ....

....

....

Take
a nap

COMPLETED ON ....

REFLECT ....

....

....

Re-read your favorite book

COMPLETED ON ....

REFLECT ....

....

....

Have a movie marathon

COMPLETED ON ....

REFLECT ....

....

....

Go for a drive.

No destination in mind

COMPLETED ON ....

REFLECT ....

....

....

Try a new podcast

COMPLETED ON ....

REFLECT ....

....

....

Put clean sheets on your bed

COMPLETED ON ....

REFLECT ....

....

....

Listen to
white noise
for five
minutes

COMPLETED ON ....

REFLECT ....

....

....

Go online window shopping

Cook
your
favorite
meal

COMPLETED ON ....

REFLECT ....

....

....

Drink your whole mug of coffee while sitting down

COMPLETED ON ....

REFLECT ....

....

....

Write yourself a love poem

COMPLETED ON ....

REFLECT ....

....

....

Make a list of your favorite hobbies.

Schedule a half hour this week to do at least one of them

COMPLETED ON ....

REFLECT ....

....

....

Set your alarm ten minutes later

COMPLETED ON ....

REFLECT ....

....

....

Take ten deep breaths

COMPLETED ON ....

REFLECT ....

....

....

Get up and walk

around the office, the house, even the room

COMPLETED ON ....

REFLECT ....

....

....

Read
in the
bathtub

COMPLETED ON ....

REFLECT ....

....

....

Take an improv class

COMPLETED ON ....

REFLECT ....

....

....

Make plans with a friend

COMPLETED ON ....

REFLECT ....

....

....

Stretch for ten minutes

COMPLETED ON ....

REFLECT ....

....

....

Get a facial

Eat your lunch outside

COMPLETED ON ....

REFLECT ....

....

....

Take yourself on a date

COMPLETED ON ....

REFLECT ....

....

....

Go for a hike

Nov 9

Smoky Mountains! Thomas, Flavia, Paola
Disfuté los colores del verano
y me desconecté del trabajo.
Feliz y relajada

Get crafty

COMPLETED ON ....

REFLECT ....

....

....

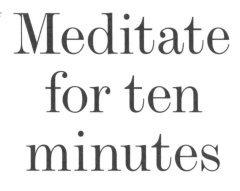

Meditate
for ten
minutes

COMPLETED ON ....

REFLECT ....

....

....

List ten things you're grateful for

COMPLETED ON ....

REFLECT ....

....

....

Plan a
dream
vacation

COMPLETED ON ....

REFLECT ....

....

....

Watch dogs at your local park

COMPLETED ON ....

REFLECT ....

....

....

Jump on the bed

COMPLETED ON ....

REFLECT ....

....

....

Try a new flavor of ice cream

COMPLETED ON ....

REFLECT ....

....

....

Give yourself a manicure

COMPLETED ON ....

REFLECT ....

....

....

Start
your novel

Wear your
favorite
color

COMPLETED ON ....

REFLECT ....

....

....

Rewatch your favorite TV show

from childhood

COMPLETED ON ....

REFLECT ....

....

....

Buy some gold star stickers

and give yourself a gold star

COMPLETED ON ....

REFLECT ....

....

....

Chew bubblegum

and blow a big bubble

COMPLETED ON ....

REFLECT ....

....

....

Slide down the slide

Order
delivery

Write a list of all the mean things you want to say,

then rip it to shreds

COMPLETED ON ....

REFLECT ....

....

....

Dance party

COMPLETED ON ....

REFLECT ....

....

....

Sing a power ballad

COMPLETED ON ....

REFLECT ....

....

....

Scroll through social media

COMPLETED ON ....

REFLECT ....

....

....

Skip work and take a day trip

COMPLETED ON ....

REFLECT ....

....

....

Go to a candy store

COMPLETED ON ....

REFLECT ....

....

....

Have a picnic

COMPLETED ON ....

REFLECT ....

....

....

Watch
a classic
movie

COMPLETED ON ....

REFLECT ....

....

....

Go to an open house

COMPLETED ON ....

REFLECT ....

....

....

Do a donut crawl

COMPLETED ON ....

REFLECT ....

....

....

Take a
bike ride

COMPLETED ON ....

REFLECT ....

....

....

Try a new exercise class

COMPLETED ON ....

REFLECT ....

....

....

Go to a museum

COMPLETED ON ....

REFLECT ....

....

....

Do a cartwheel

COMPLETED ON ....

REFLECT ....

....

....

Do your favorite things

from childhood

COMPLETED ON ....

REFLECT ....

....

....

Write yourself a thank-you note

COMPLETED ON ....

REFLECT ....

....

....

Try a new makeup style

COMPLETED ON ....

REFLECT ....

....

....

Buy a
new plant

COMPLETED ON ....

REFLECT ....

....

....

Splurge on a fancy chocolate bar

COMPLETED ON ....

REFLECT ....

....

....

Take yourself out for a nice meal

COMPLETED ON ....

REFLECT ....

....

....

Watch videos on your laptop in bed

COMPLETED ON ....

REFLECT ....

....

....

Craft
something

COMPLETED ON ....

REFLECT ....

....

....

Take a fun, silly quiz online

COMPLETED ON ....

REFLECT ....

....

....

Read
a book

COMPLETED ON ....

REFLECT ....

....

....

Hike
to the top
of a hill

and look at the view

COMPLETED ON ....

REFLECT ....

....

....

Linger over the makeup counter

Enjoy an at-home spa day

COMPLETED ON ....

REFLECT ....

....

....

Write actual letters to friends

COMPLETED ON ....

REFLECT ....

....

....

Print out and frame photos

COMPLETED ON ....

REFLECT ....

....

....

Binge-watch something

COMPLETED ON ....

REFLECT ....

....

....

Go paddle-boating

COMPLETED ON ....

REFLECT ....

....

....

Invent a
cocktail

Make an ambitious recipe

COMPLETED ON ....

REFLECT ....

....

....

Make your favorite snack

Replace
the buttons
on a jacket
with something more fabulous

COMPLETED ON ....

REFLECT ....

....

....

Clean out
the closet

COMPLETED ON ....

REFLECT ....

....

....

Treat yourself to a mani-pedi

COMPLETED ON ....

REFLECT ....

....

....

Get a massage

Make plans to grab a drink with a friend

COMPLETED ON ....

REFLECT ....

....

....

Garden

COMPLETED ON ....

REFLECT ....

....

....

Lay in
the sun

COMPLETED ON ....

REFLECT ....

....

....

Buy yourself flowers

COMPLETED ON ....

REFLECT ....

....

....

Use an aromatherapy eye pillow

for a ten minute rest

COMPLETED ON ....

REFLECT ....

....

....

Enjoy a mug of hot chocolate

COMPLETED ON ....

REFLECT ....

....

....

Go for an ice cream break

in the middle of the work day

COMPLETED ON ....

REFLECT ....

....

....

Walk
to work

COMPLETED ON ....

REFLECT ....

....

....

Spend a lazy Sunday at home

with no plans

COMPLETED ON ....

REFLECT ....

....

....

Knit
a scarf

COMPLETED ON ....

REFLECT ....

....

....

Take a hot bath

COMPLETED ON ....

REFLECT ....

....

....

Make pancakes for dinner

Buy yourself a new pen

for your journal

COMPLETED ON ....

REFLECT ....

....

....

Get a haircut

COMPLETED ON ....

REFLECT ....

....

....

Learn to do a handstand

COMPLETED ON ....

REFLECT ....

....

....

Drink a tall glass of water

COMPLETED ON ....

REFLECT ....

....

....

Savor
a piece of
seasonal
fruit

COMPLETED ON ....

REFLECT ....

....

....

Go
outside

COMPLETED ON ....

REFLECT ....

....

....

Make a meal for yourself

COMPLETED ON ....

REFLECT ....

....

....

Write down three things you do really well

COMPLETED ON ....

REFLECT ....

....

....

Look
at art

COMPLETED ON ....

REFLECT ....

....

....

Linger over the Sunday paper

Move
your body

COMPLETED ON ....

REFLECT ....

....

....

Read old emails or letters

from friends and family

COMPLETED ON ....

REFLECT ....

....

....

Make something with your hands

COMPLETED ON ....

REFLECT ....

....

....

Make a list of five things you've accomplished

COMPLETED ON ....

REFLECT ....

....

....

Write down five reasons that you are awesome

COMPLETED ON ....

REFLECT ....

....

....

Read
poetry

COMPLETED ON ....

REFLECT ....

....

....

Find a good spot to people watch

COMPLETED ON ....

REFLECT ....

....

....

Buy
yourself
lunch

COMPLETED ON ....

REFLECT ....

....

....

Make some art

COMPLETED ON ....

REFLECT ....

....

....

Notice people's different design sense

COMPLETED ON ....

REFLECT ....

....

....

Look at
old
photos

COMPLETED ON ....

REFLECT ....

....

....

Color in
a coloring
book

COMPLETED ON ....

REFLECT ....

....

....

Revisit
an old
hobby

COMPLETED ON ....

REFLECT ....

....

....

Walk
among
trees

COMPLETED ON ....

REFLECT ....

....

....

Watch a
sad movie

and have a good cry

COMPLETED ON ....

REFLECT ....

....

....

Swing
on a
swing set

Buy something cozy

for your home

COMPLETED ON ....

REFLECT ....

....

....

Watch the sunset

COMPLETED ON ....

REFLECT ....

....

....

Give yourself a head massage

Take a different route

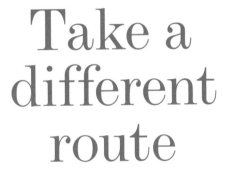

COMPLETED ON ....

REFLECT ....

....

....

List your worries on a piece of paper.

Then crumple it up and throw it away

COMPLETED ON ....

REFLECT ....

....

....

List three things that you're proud of

COMPLETED ON ....

REFLECT ....

....

....

Smell something delicious

COMPLETED ON ....

REFLECT ....

....

....

Shop
for a killer
new outfit

COMPLETED ON ....

REFLECT ....

....

....

Take a yoga class.

Or try a few poses at home

COMPLETED ON ....

REFLECT ....

....

....

Plan a weekend getaway and go

COMPLETED ON ....

REFLECT ....

....

....

Text a friend or family member

Pull out an old favorite album

COMPLETED ON ....

REFLECT ....

....

....

Listen to an episode of your favorite podcast

COMPLETED ON ....

REFLECT ....

....

....

Eat
a cookie

COMPLETED ON ....

REFLECT ....

....

....

Journal

COMPLETED ON ....

REFLECT ....

....

....

Hit the snooze button.

Twice

COMPLETED ON ....

REFLECT ....

....

....

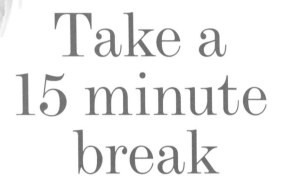

Take a 15 minute break

COMPLETED ON ....

REFLECT ....

....

....

Go for
a run

COMPLETED ON ....

REFLECT ....

....

....

Drink
a hot cup
of tea

COMPLETED ON ....

REFLECT ....

....

....

Eat something green

COMPLETED ON ....

REFLECT ....

....

....

Put on your favorite outfit

COMPLETED ON ....

REFLECT ....

....

....

Wear
crazy socks

COMPLETED ON ....

REFLECT ....

....

....

Light your favorite candle

COMPLETED ON ....

REFLECT ....

....

....

Make faces in the mirror

COMPLETED ON ....

REFLECT ....

....

....

Take a long shower

COMPLETED ON ....

REFLECT ....

....

....

Read a
webcomic

COMPLETED ON ....

REFLECT ....

....

....

Listen

to an inspirational speech

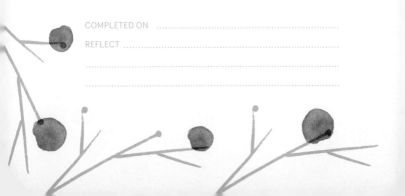

Watch the clouds

COMPLETED ON ....

REFLECT ....

....

....

Spritz your favorite smell

COMPLETED ON ....

REFLECT ....

....

....

Close your eyes and day- dream

COMPLETED ON ....

REFLECT ....

....

....

Stop and
smell the
flowers

COMPLETED ON ....

REFLECT ....

....

....

Use essential oils

COMPLETED ON ....

REFLECT ....

....

....

Change into your pajamas

COMPLETED ON ....

REFLECT ....

....

....

Lie down for ten minutes

COMPLETED ON ....

REFLECT ....

....

....

Do a crossword puzzle

COMPLETED ON ....

REFLECT ....

....

....

Break out a jigsaw puzzle

COMPLETED ON ....

REFLECT ....

....

....

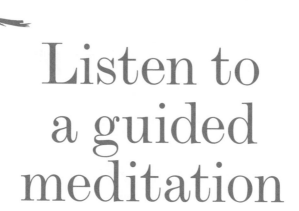

Listen to a guided meditation

COMPLETED ON ....

REFLECT ....

....

....

Give yourself a foot massage

with a tennis ball

COMPLETED ON ....

REFLECT ....

....

....

Get up early and watch a sunrise

COMPLETED ON ....

REFLECT ....

....

....

Break out some watercolors

COMPLETED ON ....

REFLECT ....

....

....

Take a picnic to the park

COMPLETED ON ....

REFLECT ....

....

....

Buy a beautiful version of a necessary tool

COMPLETED ON ....

REFLECT ....

....

....

Try a new recipe

COMPLETED ON ....

REFLECT ....

....

....

Sip your favorite cocktail

Skip
rocks

Read a book you liked as a kid

COMPLETED ON ....

REFLECT ....

....

....

Walk around a botanical garden

COMPLETED ON ....

REFLECT ....

....

....

Watch a comedy special

COMPLETED ON ....

REFLECT ....

....

....

Go to bed without setting the alarm

COMPLETED ON ....

REFLECT ....

....

....

Go to
the local
library

to find some quiet

COMPLETED ON ....

REFLECT ....

....

....

Do a little research

about something you're interested in

COMPLETED ON ....

REFLECT ....

....

....

Play a video game

COMPLETED ON ....

REFLECT ....

....

....

Do a sage smudging ritual

COMPLETED ON ....

REFLECT ....

....

....

Complain
to
someone

COMPLETED ON ....

REFLECT ....

....

....

Play dress up in your closet

COMPLETED ON ....

REFLECT ....

....

....

Pretend to be an art critic

COMPLETED ON ....

REFLECT ....

....

....

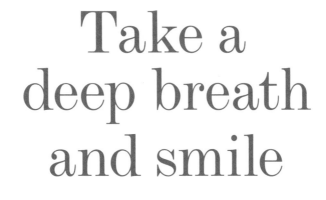

Take a deep breath and smile

COMPLETED ON ....

REFLECT ....

....

....

Watch
cartoons

COMPLETED ON ....

REFLECT ....

....

....

Take $20 to the thrift shop

COMPLETED ON ....

REFLECT ....

....

....

Walk around a flea market

COMPLETED ON ....

REFLECT ....

....

....

Revisit a favorite cookbook

COMPLETED ON ....

REFLECT ....

....

....

Go to the grocery store and

only buy
fun things

COMPLETED ON ....

REFLECT ....

....

....

Put on a
face mask

Try a
new beer

COMPLETED ON ....

REFLECT ....

....

....

Buy some fancy new stationery

COMPLETED ON ....

REFLECT ....

....

....

Crank the radio and sing along

COMPLETED ON ....

REFLECT ....

....

....

Outsource
your chores.

Use that time to take yourself out

COMPLETED ON ....

REFLECT ....

....

....

Explore a farmers' market

COMPLETED ON ....

REFLECT ....

....

....

Shop for fancy new bedding

COMPLETED ON ....

REFLECT ....

....

....

Book a staycation

COMPLETED ON ....

REFLECT ....

....

....

Use a delicious smelling body scrub

in the shower

COMPLETED ON ....

REFLECT ....

....

....

Make a list of local bakeries

and try a new one every week

COMPLETED ON ....

REFLECT ....

....

....

Bring your book to a coffee shop

COMPLETED ON ....

REFLECT ....

....

....

Sign up for a 30-day special

at a local gym

COMPLETED ON ....

REFLECT ....

....

....

Schedule a 15-minute break

COMPLETED ON ....

REFLECT ....

....

....

Read a fashion magazine

COMPLETED ON ....

REFLECT ....

....

....

Hang out
by the
pool

COMPLETED ON ....

REFLECT ....

....

....

Wake up
20 minutes
early

and enjoy the quiet

COMPLETED ON ....

REFLECT ....

....

....

Meet a
friend
for coffee

COMPLETED ON ....

REFLECT ....

....

....

Turn off your phone after dinner.

Don't turn it on again until the next morning

COMPLETED ON ....

REFLECT ....

....

....

Write
a poem

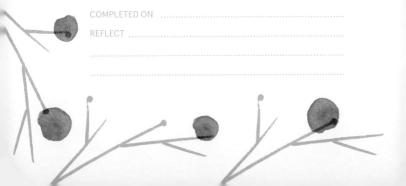

COMPLETED ON ....

REFLECT ....

....

....

Buy cute underwear

COMPLETED ON ....

REFLECT ....

....

....

Go for
a swim

COMPLETED ON ....

REFLECT ....

....

....

Go out for afternoon tea

COMPLETED ON ....

REFLECT ....

....

....

Go mini golfing

COMPLETED ON ....

REFLECT ....

....

....

Do
nothing

Get a
blowout

COMPLETED ON ....

REFLECT ....

....

....

Learn to paint

COMPLETED ON ....

REFLECT ....

....

....

Look in the mirror

and tell yourself you look beautiful

COMPLETED ON ....

REFLECT ....

....

....

Do something touristy

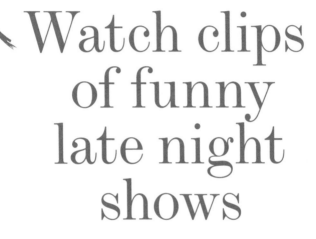

Watch clips of funny late night shows

COMPLETED ON ....

REFLECT ....

....

....

Plan
a dream
date

COMPLETED ON ....

REFLECT ....

....

....

Draw a foot bath

Practice calligraphy

COMPLETED ON ....

REFLECT ....

....

....

Splurge on skincare products

COMPLETED ON ....

REFLECT ....

....

....

Make a fancy cheese plate

COMPLETED ON ....

REFLECT ....

....

....

Get a free or low-cost makeover

at a makeup counter

COMPLETED ON ....

REFLECT ....

....

....

Buy a paperback romance novel

COMPLETED ON ....

REFLECT ....

....

....

Download ten new songs

COMPLETED ON ....

REFLECT ....

....

....

Treat yourself to a smoothie

COMPLETED ON ....

REFLECT ....

....

....

Call someone

just to check in

COMPLETED ON ....

REFLECT ....

....

....

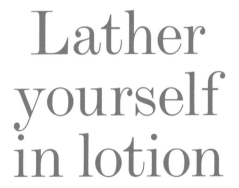

Lather
yourself
in lotion

COMPLETED ON ....

REFLECT ....

....

....

Blow
bubbles

Research
a new
career

COMPLETED ON ....

REFLECT ....

....

....

Design
your dream
home

Shred
old
documents

COMPLETED ON ....

REFLECT ....

....

....

Buy break-and-bake cookies and

bake two for yourself.

Stash the rest in the freezer

COMPLETED ON ....

REFLECT ....

....

....

Wander
around

a local garden center

COMPLETED ON ....

REFLECT ....

....

....

Buy a bunch of balloons

COMPLETED ON ....

REFLECT ....

....

....

Crochet a hat

Finger-paint

COMPLETED ON ....

REFLECT ....

....

....

Sketch
from a
picture

Try the free samples

at the grocery store

COMPLETED ON ....

REFLECT ....

....

....

Build a
pillow fort

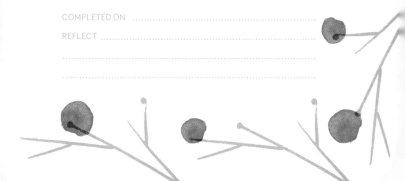

COMPLETED ON ....

REFLECT ....

....

....

Set up a hammock

COMPLETED ON ....

REFLECT ....

....

....

Walk around barefoot

Cuddle up in blankets

COMPLETED ON ....

REFLECT ....

....

....

Dunk cookies in milk

COMPLETED ON ....

REFLECT ....

....

....

Go
stargazing

COMPLETED ON ....

REFLECT ....

....

....

Make a frozen pizza

COMPLETED ON ....

REFLECT ....

....

....

Make
buttered
toast

Visit a petting zoo

COMPLETED ON ....

REFLECT ....

....

....

Draw a
mandala

COMPLETED ON ....

REFLECT ....

....

....

Shoot
some
hoops

COMPLETED ON ....

REFLECT ....

....

....

Eat
popcorn for
dinner

COMPLETED ON ....

REFLECT ....

....

....

Do a tarot reading

COMPLETED ON ....

REFLECT ....

....

....

Pet
a cat

Go to a concert

COMPLETED ON ....

REFLECT ....
....
....

Write your favorite celebrity or politician fan mail

COMPLETED ON ....

REFLECT ....

....

....

Volunteer

at a local organization

COMPLETED ON ....

REFLECT ....

....

....

Make a collage

COMPLETED ON ....

REFLECT ....

....

....

Bake a cake

and eat it straight from the pan

COMPLETED ON ....

REFLECT ....

....

....

Drink
a beer

in the shower

COMPLETED ON ....

REFLECT ....

....

....

Feed
the ducks

COMPLETED ON ....

REFLECT ....

....

....

Put on a face mask

while watching your favorite show

COMPLETED ON ....

REFLECT ....

....

....

Pick
yourself a
bouquet

COMPLETED ON ....

REFLECT ....

....

....

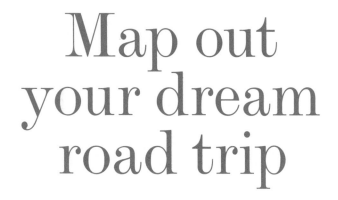

Map out
your dream
road trip

COMPLETED ON ....

REFLECT ....

....

....

Eat dessert for breakfast

COMPLETED ON ....

REFLECT ....

....

....

Sketch a
self-portrait

COMPLETED ON ....

REFLECT ....

....

....

List the top ten places you'd like to travel to

Write yourself a letter

to open in five years

COMPLETED ON ....

REFLECT ....

....

....

Walk

through the park

COMPLETED ON ....

REFLECT ....

....

....

Wash your face

COMPLETED ON ....

REFLECT ....

....

....

Look
out the
window

Put on self-tanner

COMPLETED ON ....

REFLECT ....

....

....

Add Epsom salts to your bath

COMPLETED ON ....

REFLECT ....

....

....

Read
ghost
stories

COMPLETED ON ....

REFLECT ....

....

....

Take $5 to the convenience store.

See what silly things you can buy

COMPLETED ON ....

REFLECT ....

....

....

See the view from the tallest building

COMPLETED ON ....

REFLECT ....

....

....

Ride
a carousel

COMPLETED ON ....

REFLECT ....

....

....

Go to the drive-in

COMPLETED ON ....

REFLECT ....

....

....

Visit
the zoo

Observe the fish at the aquarium

COMPLETED ON ....

REFLECT ....

....

....

Bird
watch

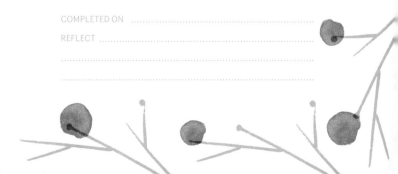

COMPLETED ON ....

REFLECT ....

....

....

Dive off the diving board

COMPLETED ON ....

REFLECT ....

....

....

Learn a dance from a music video

COMPLETED ON ....

REFLECT ....

....

....

Buy a lottery ticket

and dream about winning

COMPLETED ON ....

REFLECT ....

....

....

Track down old friends

and send one an email

COMPLETED ON ....

REFLECT ....

....

....

Go fishing

COMPLETED ON ....

REFLECT ....

....

....

Karaoke.

Bring some friends with you

COMPLETED ON ....

REFLECT ....

....

....

Call your mom

COMPLETED ON ....

REFLECT ....

....

....

Watch a baseball game

COMPLETED ON ....

REFLECT ....

....

....

Kick around a soccer ball

COMPLETED ON ....

REFLECT ....

....

....

Build a house of cards

COMPLETED ON ....

REFLECT ....

....

....

Make s'mores

in the microwave

COMPLETED ON ....

REFLECT ....

....

....

Cash in
your coins

and buy yourself a treat

COMPLETED ON ....

REFLECT ....

....

....

Take a life drawing class

COMPLETED ON ....

REFLECT ....

....

....

Make a visual journal of your day

COMPLETED ON ....

REFLECT ....

....

....

Lean on someone

COMPLETED ON ....

REFLECT ....

....

....

Make
a zine

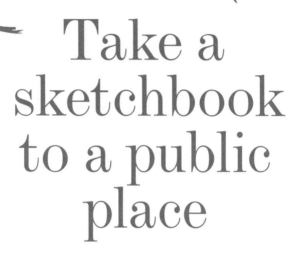

Take a sketchbook to a public place

COMPLETED ON ....

REFLECT ....

....

....

Serenade
yourself in
the mirror

COMPLETED ON ....

REFLECT ....

....

....

Create
a mood
board

to express yourself

COMPLETED ON ....

REFLECT ....

....

....

Check out a local tourist attraction

COMPLETED ON ....

REFLECT ....

....

....

Explore unusual markets in your town

and try something new

COMPLETED ON ....

REFLECT ....

....

....

Paint
your nails

a fun and flashy color

COMPLETED ON ....

REFLECT ....

....

....

Go out dancing

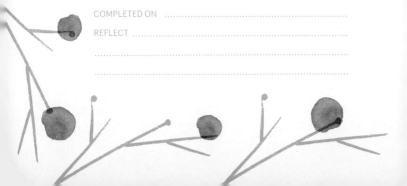

COMPLETED ON ....

REFLECT ....

....

....

Go beach combing

COMPLETED ON ....

REFLECT ....

....

....

Take time to watch the waves roll in

COMPLETED ON ....

REFLECT ....

....

....

Have breakfast for dinner

Find a rose garden

and smell the roses

COMPLETED ON ....

REFLECT ....

....

....

Get a palm reading

Eat a cupcake

COMPLETED ON ....

REFLECT ....

....

....

Try
acupuncture

COMPLETED ON ....

REFLECT ....

....

....

Soak in a hot tub

COMPLETED ON ....

REFLECT ....

....

....

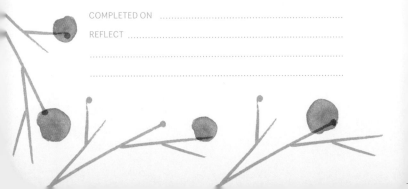

Relax in a sauna or steam room

COMPLETED ON ....

REFLECT ....

....

....

Put cold cucumber slices on your eyes

COMPLETED ON ....

REFLECT ....

....

....

Bake
fresh
bread

COMPLETED ON ....

REFLECT ....

....

....

Write a new ending

to a book

COMPLETED ON ....

REFLECT ....

....

....

Draw with sidewalk chalk

COMPLETED ON ....

REFLECT ....

....

....

Yell
as loud as
you can

COMPLETED ON ....

REFLECT ....

....

....

Listen
to a shell

COMPLETED ON ....

REFLECT ....

....

....

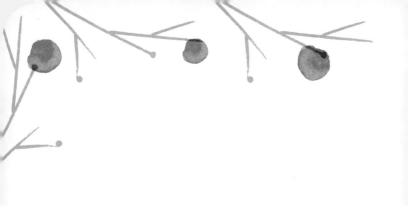

Fold
origami

COMPLETED ON ....

REFLECT ....

....

....

Buy a
fun app

COMPLETED ON ....

REFLECT ....

....

....

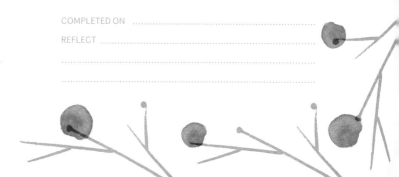

Learn the lyrics to a favorite song

COMPLETED ON ....

REFLECT ....

....

....

Make a friendship bracelet

Play
pinball

COMPLETED ON ....

REFLECT ....

....

....

Organize
your desk

COMPLETED ON ....

REFLECT ....

....

....

Watch a
makeup
tutorial

and try to recreate it

COMPLETED ON ....

REFLECT ....

....

....

Topple
dominos

Play
solitaire

COMPLETED ON ....

REFLECT ....

....

....

Dye
your hair

COMPLETED ON ....

REFLECT ....

....

....

Sit
on a park
bench

COMPLETED ON ....

REFLECT ....

....

....

Rent a convertible

COMPLETED ON ....

REFLECT ....

....

....

Do a
sudoku
puzzle

Schedule
a future
treat

COMPLETED ON ....

REFLECT ....

....

....

Make a dinner reservation

somewhere new

COMPLETED ON ....

REFLECT ....

....

....

Go out to your favorite restaurant

COMPLETED ON ....

REFLECT ....

....

....

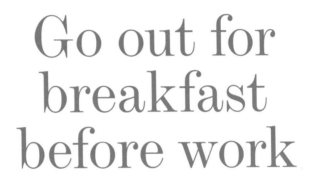

Go out for breakfast before work

COMPLETED ON ....

REFLECT ....

....

....

Draw your
self-portrait

COMPLETED ON ....

REFLECT ....

....

....

Lean against a tree

COMPLETED ON ....

REFLECT ....

....

....

Lie on
your back

and look up at the sky

COMPLETED ON ....

REFLECT ....

....

....

Buy a funny postcard

and mail it to someone

COMPLETED ON ....

REFLECT ....

....

....

Browse the travel section

of a bookstore

COMPLETED ON ....

REFLECT ....

....

....

Pick up a
newspaper

COMPLETED ON ....

REFLECT ....

....

....

Do a DIY project

COMPLETED ON ....

REFLECT ....

....

....

Float
down a
river

Research
your family
history

COMPLETED ON ....

REFLECT ....

....

....

Learn a few words in a foreign language

COMPLETED ON ....

REFLECT ....

....

....

Take photos on your phone

COMPLETED ON ....

REFLECT ....

....

....

Do
Tai Chi

Read positive quotes

COMPLETED ON ....

REFLECT ....

....

....

Laugh
out loud

COMPLETED ON ....

REFLECT ....

....

....

Rub your temples

to relieve tension

Make a card for a friend

COMPLETED ON ....

REFLECT ....

....

....

Try a crazy potato chip flavor

COMPLETED ON ....

REFLECT ....

....

....

Give someone a hug.

You'll get one in return

COMPLETED ON ....

REFLECT ....

....

....

Pick your own fruit

COMPLETED ON ....

REFLECT ....

....

....

Scream into a pillow

COMPLETED ON ....

REFLECT ....

....

....

Declutter
your space

Fill out
Mad Libs

What else can you do?

COMPLETED ON ....

REFLECT ....

....

....

What else can you do?

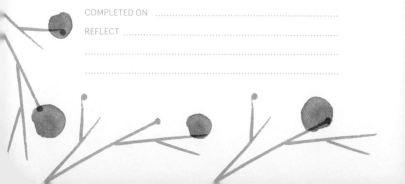

COMPLETED ON ....

REFLECT ....

....

....

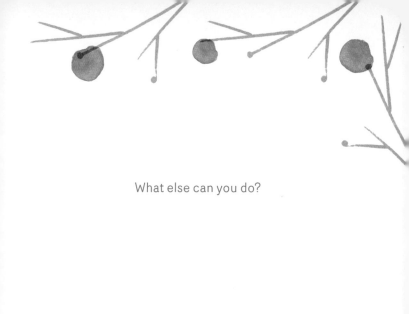

What else can you do?

COMPLETED ON ....

REFLECT ....

....

....

What else can you do?

COMPLETED ON ....

REFLECT ....

....

....

What else can you do?

COMPLETED ON ....

REFLECT ....

....

....

What else can you do?

COMPLETED ON ....

REFLECT ....

....

....

What else can you do?

COMPLETED ON ....

REFLECT ....

....

....

What else can you do?

COMPLETED ON ....

REFLECT ....

....

....

What else can you do?

What else can you do?

COMPLETED ON ....

REFLECT ....

....

....

What else can you do?

COMPLETED ON ....

REFLECT ....

....

....